PREFACE: STEPPING INTO PRAYER
BY DR. ARNOLD EISEN
CHANCELLOR, JEWISH THEOLOGICAL SEMINARY

Tefilah does not come easily to most contemporary Jews. Standing before God; sensing God's presence; speaking to God in thanksgiving, petition or praise; hearing God speak in return – these are among the most difficult acts that our tradition invites Jewish adults in our generation to perform. They can also be among the most rewarding. Raise your voice in song along with the members of your community, experience deeper connection to your tradition and your family, take advantage of moments of silence and peace that are rarely available in the rush of daily obligation – and you know that *tefilah* can be a source of Meaning at once joyous and profound.

That is why I am honored and pleased, as Chancellor of JTS, to welcome you to the FJMC's Learners' and Interpretation *minyan* curriculum. This guide wisely meets people where they are. It does not assume knowledge of or comfort with the synagogue service, and yet has much to offer even veteran shul-goers. You will find helpful hints to synagogue choreography ("we rise here"), suggestions that may enhance your experience of *tefilah* ("some find that humming a *niggun* during this section is meaningful"), and precious reassurance that your personal questions about prayer are widely-shared ("you don't need to say everything!") Ample room is left for individual prayer-leaders and participants to supply their own suggestions, interpretations, *kavanot* and pedagogy.

New-comers to *tefilah* often mistakenly believe that everyone else in the room experiences no challenges that get in the way of prayer: no theological difficulties, no distraction or self-consciousness, no restlessness after sitting for hours. It's important to dispel that misunderstanding at the outset through honest conversation. In the same way, everyone in a prayer-community benefits from frank discussion of what brings particular individuals to *shul* that day over and above the mitzvah itself: specific reasons for gratitude or anxiety, desire for connection or atonement, a prayer for healing or the need to say *kaddish* for a loved one. Jewish prayer has remained meaningful over many centuries because Jewish prayers fill the words with ever new meaning. The process is more remarkable still – and more satisfying – because if often takes place in a synagogue setting, where each of us sits and chants alongside others who bring very different concerns, intentions and emotions to their *tefilah*. We come together in *tefilah* in ways we do not elsewhere – and, if it works right, we leave synagogue with the sense that we really have connected more deeply to God (however we understand the divine), to one another, and to ourselves.

I am not always riveted by the service of the synagogue, but I am nearly always glad to be there, grateful for the age-old words, the music of many generations, the precious moments of silence, and the company of my community. On behalf of my colleagues at JTS – dedicated to the strengthening of Jewish traditions such as *tefilah,* Jewish lives and Jewish communities, I wish you great fulfillment as we walk together on the Jewish journey that lasts a life-time.

Portions of this preface were adapted from "Conservative Judaism Today and Tomorrow" published in 2014 by the Jewish Theological Seminary.

ABOUT THE AUTHORS

Bob Braitman and Norm Kurtz are both past international Presidents of the Federation of Jewish Men's Clubs, Inc. (FJMC). Bob is a practicing physician specializing in Pediatric and Adolescent medicine and serves as a *mohel* in New England. He has been married to Bonnie Gordon for nearly 40 years. Norm, an attorney, lives in Chicago and has been married to Joan for a similar amount of time. Bob was instrumental in creating a model teaching Shabbat morning service at the New England FJMC annual retreat. Norm created and for the last four years piloted an "Interpretive service" in his synagogue.

Both men have a passion for making prayer more accessible and meaningful.

Bob is responsible for the FJMC "Hearing Men's Voices" initiative a publication and programmatic vehicle to involve Jewish men in Jewish life: Norm, for the creation of the Joel S. Geffen Leadership Development Institute. Both Norm and Bob were the instrumental in the creation of *CJ: Voices of Conservative/Masorti* Judaism, a joint project with the United Synagogue and the Women's League. Both men served as Chairs of the Leadership Council of Conservative Judaism.

TABLE OF CONTENTS

PREFACE: STEPPING INTO PRAYER   3
By Dr. Arnold Eisen
Chancellor, Jewish Theological Seminary

ABOUT THE AUTHORS   4

INTRODUCTION   6
Creating Opportunities for Meaningful *Shabbat Tefilah*:
A Facilitator's Guide

THE FRAMEWORK   7

SERVICE MODELS   10

THE LEARNER'S SERVICE SERIES   11
By Robert E. Braitman, M.D.

THE INTERPRETIVE/EXPERIENTIAL SERVICE   31
By Norman Kurtz

APPENDIX   38

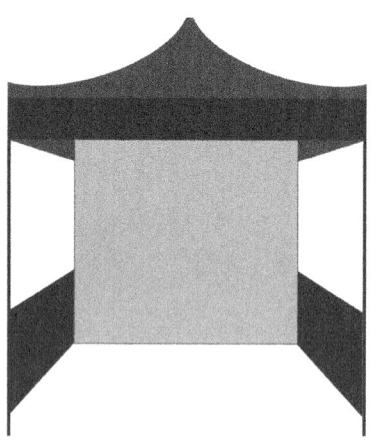

INTRODUCTION
CREATING OPPORTUNITIES FOR MEANINGFUL *SHABBAT TEFILAH*:
A FACILITATOR'S GUIDE

Why are the pews so empty on *Shabbat* morning? When asked, many people change the subject or simply reply that *Shabbat* morning prayer in the synagogue is not for them. The reasons?

- Other activities have a higher priority
- Other activities may seem to provide more "spiritual" meaning (like a walk in the woods) than three hours in shul.
- The Shabbat prayer experience is not meaningful to them because:

  > They can't read Hebrew
  > They don't understand the prayers
  > They don't believe in God, so how can they pray?
  > Services are too long and too boring
  > They don't know what's going on
  > And so on…

Even for those who do attend *Shabbat* services regularly, some of these responses may ring true. This is not a simple problem. Many congregational leaders have been trying to solve it for years, and we will share some of that wisdom here.

When we participate in an activity, whether attending the theater, visiting a museum, playing golf or even getting a haircut, we enter the venue with clear expectations of what we expect to gain from the experience. Yet very few of us have thought about or articulated our expectations for the *Shabbat* morning synagogue experience. It would be a fair assumption that many of us do not have a sufficient skill set to make that activity meaningful and worthwhile. But, what can we do about it?

As leaders of our synagogues, let's turn the tables and ask ourselves as the "providers" of these services, how we would envision a more satisfying outcome for those in attendance? How can we make the experience more moving, more challenging, more inspiring? How can we make this experience more educational, more motivational, more comforting? How can we make being part of a *Shabbat* community more enriching?

The answer of course is that everyone will have a different experience and a different outcome. By focusing on some specific goals, however, we can fine-tune the service experience in our communities. We are going to look at how the current service model can be modified. We will show how one or more alternative parallel experiences can be offered. There are a variety of tools at our disposal and we are going to

HOW TO USE THIS GUIDE

evaluate some of them.

This guide is designed for those who are interested in enhancing the experience of *tefilah* (prayer) in their communities. Recognizing that each community is different, this manual has been designed to encourage the exploration and implementation of alternatives to the status quo. The goal is to involve men and women in the *Shabbat* worship experience who, for a variety of reasons, have not found meaning in their previous experiences in the sanctuary.

The manual is organized in three sections:

- The Framework
- Service models: the Learner's service and the Interpretive/Experiential Service
- Resources to enhance your programming

We've included these two models that have proven track records as well as practical advice on how to get started. Feel free to use these models or adapt them to what works best in your own community. You will notice that there is considerable overlap between these models. Again, take what is most applicable to your setting and make it your own.

This guide provides a road map for you, the synagogue's lay leaders, to encourage congregants who are not currently attending services to take another look at what is offered in your community. Because there are scant resources about implementing programs to make communal prayer meaningful, we have created this guide to supplement the many books and other resources about prayer that have already been published.

These materials are offered as just a beginning. Some excellent publications that are available to you to enhance your programming are listed at the end.

THE FRAMEWORK

At the beginning of this process there are four considerations to take into account.

1. Identify the key players in the community, the decision makers, who have to be supporting the initiative. At the very least, the synagogue's executive committee cannot be against it. There are often other key players, and be sure to consider who they may be.

2. Synagogue professionals – the Rabbi, *Hazzan,* Ritual Director, Education Director and Executive Director all must be on board.

3. What are the obstacles to implementation? Among other factors, inertia is a frequent problem. Many people prefer the status quo. In this situation, because ritual committees are often populated by regular attendees who are satisfied with the status quo, the need for and benefit of alternative services may not be apparent to them.

4. Before bringing a proposal to the board or ritual committee, identify what space you propose using. Once you get the green light, be sure to reserve this space on the master calendar so the staff can do set up and clean up.

Once there is sign-off and the planning can begin in earnest, there are two critical factors to spend time planning for. First, make sure to tailor your teachings to the demographic of those who are attending your service. Comments that are meaningful to one group may not resonate in the same way with another. And finally, make sure to identify and train the leaders of these alternative experiences. There are many motivated lay members in every community who can lead these sessions.

Key principles for all services

- The goal of every prayer experience should be that the participants leave the service somehow changed.

- Prayer is not just a process of recitation.

- Prayer is intended to be a transformative and transcendent experience.

- Many participants need to be "re-wired" to experience the potential of prayer.

- Don't underestimate the power of creating a warm, safe and friendly environment. A hug, handshake, high-five and friendly welcome can be a game-changer.

- Plan your time carefully. Decide in advance the balance between "teaching" and "doing". Be realistic as to how much material you can include.

- Be careful to translate or explain Hebrew (or Yiddish) terms the first time you use them. Words, like *"minyan"*, *"daven"*, *drash*, etc. may not be familiar to everyone.

Key qualities required of the service leaders

Passion. First and foremost, leaders of these services must themselves have a love of *Shabbat* and a passion for tefilah and Torah study. This is not just a subject to be taught. Attendees will absorb that passion as they become engaged the experience.

Knowledge. Understanding the *tefilah* itself and the specific skills that are required is essential. Leaders should be comfortable in reading the Hebrew liturgy and have sufficient musical ability to model the *nusakh* (the melodic style specific to Shabbat morning). Leaders must have good working knowledge of the service and service structure to be able to answer participant questions in a meaningful way.

Public Speaking/Teaching Skills. Whether a learner's service or an alternative service, we may view them as if they were liturgical theater that requires the leaders to be charismatic and know how to involve and transform their "audience".

Creativity. This manual provides a blueprint or template. Each leader will need to add his or her own personality, material and flair.

Flexibility. Not everything works as smoothly as planned. Leaders must be flexible enough to spend more or less time on various aspects of the service, as their sense of that specific group dictates. Leaders must be able to think on their feet.

The goals of these alternate services:

Comfort. To provide attendees with a level of comfort when they attend a *Shabbat* morning service. To provide members of our communities with a portal to *Shabbat* morning prayer, one that is welcoming, comfortable, meaningful, educational, spiritual and based on our customs and traditions.

Knowledge. To give attendees the basic information that they need to understand what happens during the service and to comprehend the meaning of the prayers.

Meaning. To provide a context for the prayer experience that resonates with their lives. Why is this experience meaningful to them? To view prayer from a variety of perspectives – God as Creator, God as Revealer, and God as a personal and caring "partner". Can religious language be beneficial even when faith and belief is in doubt?

Motivation. To either return and become a part of the congregation's main service or to continue attending the alternate services. To foster potentially stimulating eye-opening, mind and heart opening receptivity to sense the wonder and grandeur that may be derived from communal Jewish prayer, particularly on *Shabbat* morning.

SERVICE MODELS

The Learner's Service Series

Overview:

- This series could be offered once or twice during the year.
- Ideally, initially plan for 6 regularly scheduled sessions.
- Each session builds on the previous one. Material presented at the previous session becomes part of the "service" next time so that by the final session, attendees are participating in a "full" service.
- Introduce *niggun* (wordless melody) - music moves the soul.
- Include a "learner's *kiddush*". This builds on the community-building that took place during the shared experience of the service, and again makes participants more comfortable with the regular congregational experience.
- Teach prayers to include the "*p'shat*" (straightforward meaning) of what is said and include a "*drash*" which provides deeper meaning for each aspect of the service. What is the prayer trying to express? What is its message? Consider your teaching technique. What works best for you and for those who are attending this learner's program? What is the balance between didactic "teaching", story-telling, *niggunim*, etc.?
- Develop a "buddy system" for attendees so that they feel comfortable when joining the main or other *Shabbat* services in the community. One of the most important components of a satisfying *Shabbat* synagogue experience is having someone you already know to share it with.

The Interpretive/Experiential Service

Overview: This is not a learners' service per se (although it can be), but rather it is a service designed for adults, regardless of whether literate in Hebrew, who wish to share community on *Shabbat* morning; who wish to have a regular *Shabbat* morning prayer experience; and who wish to improve their understanding of *Shabbat*, of prayer and of Torah by participating in a prayer service on regular basis on *Shabbat* morning. This is designed to be offered as an ongoing alternative to the main congregational service. Attendees may continue to attend this alternate service or the traditional service as they like.

A Brief History:

Much of this material was developed for the annual retreat organized by the New England Region of FJMC. The weekend at Camp Ramah enables men to join together for prayer, study and recreation. It became clear that many of us were lost and otherwise unable to participate in the *davening* at camp so we proposed an alternate service that would allow time to teach about the liturgy, etc. Initially there was some push-back from the committee. There was concern that this would split the group and reduce participation. In the years since its introduction the opposite has been true. Attendance at all services at the retreat has increased as well. In addition, many men have returned to their communities inspired to learn, to participate and indeed to become leaders at their synagogues.

THE LEARNER'S SERVICE SERIES

BY ROBERT E. BRAITMAN, M.D.

General Comments:

Allow 2 hours for each session (Be flexible. Time should match goals for the session and needs of the community). Try to end around the same time as the main service in case people want to carpool to *shul* with participants in that service.

Begin each session by allowing attendees to introduce themselves (if group size is conducive). Ask some to comment on why they are attending the learner's service, although you may need to limit this if time is a factor. [Possible answers are listed in the section for Session 1. Some attendees may be using the learner's experience as an entry point into *tefilah* more generally.]

Review the order of the service each time. Prepare a handout keyed to the siddur used by your community. A sample is in the Appendix.

Include explanations of choreography – standing, sitting, bowing and shuffling, making sure to teach when we bow so people will feel like they fit in more when they attend the main services of the synagogue.

Discuss and demonstrate the practice of unique *nusakhot* for various sections, etc. (leaders should be comfortable in reading the Hebrew of the liturgy and have sufficient musical ability to model the *nusakh*).

Introduction and a *kavanah* for each section of the Service will help learners understand each section.

Use *niggunim*. It helps people who don't know Hebrew to feel included. Take care to introduce only one new *niggun* per session and use it more than once so participants can learn it.

Use it once in the next session to remind people. By the end of the series they will have a repertoire of melodies they've learned.

Each session of this series will focus on one section of the service. Start the session with an icebreaker (see below), discuss the new section in detail and then lead the group in prayer from the beginning with a modified but complete service (see below for guidelines). Sessions build on each other.

Encourage questions but keep discussion on topic.

Keep the goal of fostering potentially stimulating eye-opening, mind-opening, heart-opening receptivity to sense the wonder and grandeur that may be derived from Jewish prayer in mind.

Consider ending each session with a private *kiddush* for attendees. This will facilitate everyone getting to know each other. Practice *Shabbat kiddush, motzi* and handwashing in this "safe" setting (As part of the "graduation" attendees will be welcomed "officially" to the congregational *kiddush* and asked to lead these blessings). Once people feel comfortable with how *kiddush* works, they will feel more included when they attend the main service on *Shabbat* and festivals.

Create a "buddy system" so that attendees have support when they join the main or other Shabbat services in the community. Sitting alone can make learners feel like they don't belong to the rest of the community.

Room Setup: Importance of Fostering a Safe and Warm Environment

Changing the seating configuration allows for participants to feel that this is a different experience.

Move chairs (if possible) to create a more intimate setting. Examples are "U" shape or circle. Leave room for access, etc.

Warm-up/Icebreaker/Mood Setting Possibilities

Teach a *niggun* and have everyone join in. Teach a new one each week for people to build up a repertoire, so when they hear the melody in another setting they will feel included.

Familiar prayers such as *modeh ani* or *ashrei* allow for easy entry to the experience.

If the synagogue has beautiful grounds, take a brief walk.

"Set the Stage" and Your Students

"Are you 'set'?" Getting "set" is preparing your students to say *heneni*, "I am ready" and to "be there" in a mental state of readiness. You create a vocabulary and a context to process the experience.

    Get learners "set," thinking and ready for the lesson
    Catch the students' attention; provide PERSONAL meaning
    Arouse curiosity
    Pose interesting questions
    Use dramatic appeal
    Create a need or interest

After reviewing the training material each session, conduct a regular Shabbat morning service (the same service each session).

Remind attendees that by learning what is in the different sections of the service each week, meaning will be added to meaning so that by the end of the series they will (hopefully) find the beauty, joy, meaning and passion that is part of this rich liturgy.

Repeat the *niggun* that was taught at the beginning of the learning part of the session.

~~

THE SERVICE FOR EACH WEEK

Focus for Session One – *Amidah* (p.16)

1. *Musaf Amidah (Haiche Kedushah)*
2. *Kaddish shalem*
3. *Ein k'eloheinu*
4. *Aleinu*
5. Mourner's *Kaddish*
6. *Adon olam*

Focus for Session Two – *The Sh'ma* (p.18)

7. *Barkhu*
8. First blessing before the *Sh'ma* read silently
9. Sing *ahava rabba*
10. Recite the *Sh'ma* declaration and the *v'ahavta* paragraph outloud, remaining two paragraphs recited silently
11. *Mi-khamokha* to end of page
12. *Shacharit Amidah* with *haiche kedushah* – a public recitation of the *Amidah* prayer until the end of the *kedushah*, at which point individuals continue to the end silently.

Focus for Session Three – *The Torah Service (p.21)*

13. Torah Service. Either the triennial reading or shorter readings. Consider including reading of English translation of some/all of portions read.
14. Teach about *Haftarah* but don't recite
15. *Ashrei*
16. Return Torah to the ark

Focus for Session Four – P'sukai D'zimra *(p.26)*

17. *Barukh she-amar*
18. *Ashrei* or Psalm 136
19. *Nishmat*
20. *Shokhen Ad* through *Yish-tabah*
21. *Kaddish*

Focus for Session Five – *Birkhot Ha-Shchar* (p.28)

Review *birchot ha-shahar* and more psalms of *p'sukei d'zimra*. Then add that portion into the service.

Focus for Session Six – *Putting It All Together (p.30)*

Go through the entire service from beginning to end. Start with a *niggun*. Consider using the *niggun* to separate portions of the service. Add some *kavanot* throughout as you see fit. Use some of the *niggunim* taught during the series for the prayers (like *El Adon* and *Adon olam*).

~~

SET THE STAGE AND PREPARE FOR *TEFILAH*

- Explore and encourage concept of "setting a goal" for your morning in shul.
- What do you want to "get out" of the experience?
- Possible answers include:
    - Comfort
    - Experience Wonder
    - Peace
    - Contemplation
    - Intellectual Stimulation
- Transformation of soul/spiritual experience.
- We pray to get onto God's frequency so that we can hear God's voice and perhaps act in God's image during the coming day.
- The world is full of the light of God, but to see it we have to open our eyes.

Praying in Hebrew

There is an emotional element that reciting a prayer in Hebrew can add to those who do not understand every word - a feeling of identification with other Jews. Is the English really more meaningful? I would argue that understanding the theme of the prayer and tuning into God's voice is more meaningful than reading every word in prayer book English. A good way to start is by using transliterations that are widely available. Many of the newer prayer books include transliterations for those parts of the service that are said or sung by the congregation. An added benefit to learning the pronunciation of the prayers in Hebrew is that when visiting synagogues elsewhere in the world, whether Israel, Italy or Argentina, one can join in the service when Hebrew prayers are recited.

~~

A FINAL GENERAL COMMENT

Be sure to teach participants that pages are announced to let you know where the prayer leader is reading, but that **you do not need to be on the same page or even within the same prayer. Teach them that it's okay to take your time, focus on a word, a phrase, a thought, that you do not need to read or say every word of the service.** The *siddur* is like a great museum. There are numerous masterpieces within but you never expect to see them all in one visit. It's okay to be on a different page from the rest of the congregation.

SESSION #1: INTRODUCTORY MATERIAL: WHY DO WE PRAY;

The *Amidah*, *Kaddish(s)*, *Adon Olam*, and the Final Section of the Service

Explain the nature of a learner's service and our method at each session:

- We will explore and discuss various prayers and service elements
- We'll take an in-depth look at one part of the service each session but experience a "complete" service each time.

A general comment to participants before beginning – reinforce at each session.

Page announcements let you know where the prayer leader is reading. **You do not need to be on the same page or even within the same prayer. Take your time, focus on a word, a phrase, a thought. You do not need to read or say every word of the service.** The *siddur* is like a great museum. There are numerous masterpieces within but you never expect to see them all in one visit.

Preparation for learning:

- *Think of a time when you've approached a parent, a teacher, an employer or supervisor.*
- *How did you prepare?*
- *How did you start the conversation?*
- *Visualize your body language*

Amidah

The cornerstone of worship, known as the *"Amidah"* (or standing prayer) is also called, "The Prayer" or *"Ha-tefilah"*. What is prayer? It is different things at different times. To exalt, rejoice; to plumb the depths of one's being, to confess, to give thanks, to pause in wonder at the mysteries of life, or simply to pray in its simplest form, to ask for something.

Each religion has its own distinctive way of communicating with and finding God. Pentecostals may speak in tongues, Buddhists meditate, and Catholics take communion. Jews find God through conversation. The *Amidah* is one of those conversations with God.

The *Amidah* consists of blessings of praise, and on weekdays of requests. On *Shabbat* the central 13 "request" blessings are replaced with paragraphs that change with each Shabbat service from Friday night, through *Shabbat shacharit*, to *musaf* and finally at *minhah*.

The spiritual experience of reciting the *Amidah* is like being in the presence of God.

Before we begin there is a verse from the psalms (*do you skip this too?*) "*Adonai* open my mouth and my lips will proclaim Your praise". Choreography: As you begin the *Amidah* you take three steps backwards and forwards. Try saying those six Hebrew words (*Adonai s'fatai tiftah u'fi yagid te-hilatekha*), one with each step forward and back, as you begin your prayer.

Choreography: You bow with bended knees three times during the *Amidah*. At the word "*barukh*" bend the knees and at the word "*atah*" bend at the waist. Stand straight for the name of God, "*Adonai*". These three times are at the beginning of the first paragraph, for the *brakha* after that, "Praised are You, Shield of Abraham", and when reciting the *brakha* in the paragraph toward the end, "Praised are You, beneficent Lord to whom all praise is due". At the beginning of the paragraph "*Modim anahnu lakh*", one bows only from the waist, not bending the knees.

The introductory blessing has the phrase "*Ha-el Ha-gadol, Ha-gibbor, V'hanorah – Eil Elyon*". Each of us should think about various aspects of God that define these characteristics.

- *Gadol*: great
- *Gibbor*: powerful
- *Norah*: awesome
- *Eil Elyon*: God most high, greater than all other powers.

The Kedushah

The *kedushah* is the poetic setting for recitation of verses from Isaiah, Ezekiel and Psalms. You are in the heavenly court. Mystics would try to ascend to heaven and come into the presence of God. We rise on our toes. You should not speak or move around the shul during the kedushah, and those who usher should close the doors at this time.

The *Musaf Amidah* makes reference to additional sacrifices that were offered on *Shabbat* only, in the paragraphs after the *kedushah* and before the *modim anakhnu lakh*.

The final blessing of the *Amidah*, "*sim shalom*", is a prayer for peace

Spend time on meditation at the end of *Amidah*. It is a meditation of *Mar Son of Ravina*, one of several suggested in the *Gemara* (Tractate B'rakhot 16b-17a). Read other examples if there is time. This one admonishes oneself to avoid the sin of *lashon hara* - slander and tale bearing. The *Talmud* places this sin in the same category as that of bloodshed. Why put this meditation here? The *Zohar* says "He who has an evil tongue, his prayers will not be heard".

Kaddish: The pause that refreshes.

Introduce the concept of the *kaddish* as an indication that we are completing a portion of the service.

Review the various forms that *kaddish* takes (full and half).

This is a good time to take a deep breath, perhaps look into yourself and spend a few minutes thinking about your family, the week just past, etc.

***Adon olam:* Not Just Musical Accompaniment for Removing the *Tallit* and Getting Ready for Lunch.**

Explore structure of the poem. It goes from grand and general descriptions of God to the very personal. Read the poem and Hebrew and English.

Teach a new melody – just about anything in 4/4 time can be used.

~~

SESSION #2: THE *SH'MA* AND THE BLESSINGS BEFORE AND AFTER

Explain the Nature of a Learner's Service and Our Method at each session:

- We will explore and discuss various prayers and service elements.
- We'll take an in-depth look at one part of the service each session but experience a "complete" service each time.

A general comment to participants before beginning – reinforce at each session.

Page announcements let you know where the prayer leader is reading. **You do not need to be on the same page or even within the same prayer. Take your time, focus on a word, a phrase, a thought. You do not need to read or say every word of the service.** The *siddur* is like a great museum. There are numerous masterpieces within but you never expect to see them all in one visit.

This Session: The *Sh'ma* and its blessings

Preparation: What is the most observed Jewish ceremony? The Passover Seder. No matter how simple or complex your ceremony at home may be, one thing is common to all. We tell our story. We recall that WE were slaves in Egypt. This ancient story never gets old.
If you were to tell your own life story, how would you begin?
Would there be a climactic crescendo in the heart of the story?

Our daily prayers tell our story as well. The "*Sh'ma* and its Blessings" section of the service begins with creation, moves to the giving of the Torah and ultimately to our redemption from Egypt. Right there in the middle is an amazing section of God's love.
Note that when talking about creating luminaries the present tense is used stressing the ideas of God's daily renewal of creation.

Barkhu – "The Call to Prayer" (compare "hear ye, hear ye"). This represents the transition from private prayer to prayer as a community

Barkhu

In the first paragraph after *barkhu* there is much talk of angels. In this prayer the angels take on the yoke of heaven, sort of a preview to the *Sh'ma* to follow. One sage says that "the ministering angels do not mention the name of the Holy One on high until Israel mentions it below." Thus Israel's praise has a cosmic significance.

Within this section is a paragraph where each word begins with a different letter of the alphabet. On *Shabbat* that paragraph is expanded into a full-fledged hymn-*eil adon*-where now the acrostic is line-by-line. Teach and practice a melody for this hymn.

The first blessing describes the heavenly lights, the sun and the moon and thanks God for creation.

The second blessing is one of the supreme expressions of love in the liturgy. Having spoken of God's relationship to the universe, we now speak of God's relationship to us. Notice the phrase "our Father, compassionate Father, ever compassionate, have compassion on us". The channel through which this love flows is the Torah.

> From Rabbi Bradley Artson: "The entire Jewish tradition is a recurring outpouring of covenantal love: God creates the world, we are told, in order to have an object to love. And if that isn't enough, God rises up against Pharaoh and brings us to freedom, because God so loves our ancestors. As if that isn't enough, God brings us to the foot of Mount Sinai and there offers us a covenantal contract, which the Rabbis tell us is a *ketubah*, a wedding contract. This *ketubah* sealing the relationship between the Jewish people and God is the very *Sefer* Torah we read from today. Ours is an ancient tradition of covenantal love."

We gather the four corners of the *tzitzit* in preparation for the *Sh'ma*. when we say "*v'havieinu l'shalom* – You bring us from the four corners of the earth". We hold them together during the entire *Sh'ma*, kissing them at the appropriate times in the third paragraph, and letting them go in the paragraph following the *Sh'ma*.

Again the declaration *Sh'ma Yisrael* that immediately follows affirms the acceptance of this gift and of the love.

It is traditional to cover one's eyes when saying the first line of the *Sh'ma*. This tradition allows you to focus intently on these 6 words with *kavanah* and without distraction.

The word *Sh'ma* is untranslatable in English. It means:
>   Listen
>   Hear
>   Reflect on
>   Understand
>   Internalize
>   Respond with *mitzvot*
>   Obey

What is "*Echad*"? "One", "Alone", "Whole"?

In the first paragraph after the declaration of *Sh'ma (v'ahavta)*, we again learn that the way to love God is by performance of *mitzvot*. What would happen if we read this paragraph as: "*Oh....if only you would love your God with all your heart, all your soul and all your might.*" Reading this way, the *Sh'ma* invites us twice daily to offer the one thing that God cannot command - because it is impossible to command - human love. Another way to look at "*ahava*" is as a behavior ("loyalty") and a feeling ("emotion/love"). Also note that the teaching of children mentioned here implies that this teaching is continuous, as you sit in the house, walk and go about your daily life. Not just in discrete classroom lessons.

The second paragraph of the *Sh'ma* talks about community responsibility. Some have argued that the *mitzvot* referred to here specifically are those referring to the land. They understand this blessing as saying that if you abuse the gift of the land you will lose it. In modern terms, this says that if you pollute the air you will suffer from climate change.

In third and final paragraph, the *tzitzit* are a reminder of God's redeeming us from slavery. They also serve as a reminder to observe the *mitzvot*. We are enjoined: *lo ta-tu-ru,* not to "pick up on "false gods. This same word is used to describe the scouts who in the same parsha returned a false and disheartening verdict about *Eretz Yisrael*. When the word "*tzitzit*" is read each of the three times, they are kissed.

What are your personal tzitzit? Your personal reminders to do the right thing?

In the next paragraph, *Emet v'yatziv*, we begin by saying *Emet*, (*spanning the entire alphabet from the letters aleph to taf with a nun in* *the middle)*. Listen to the Hebrew. The power of this prayer is in the repetition (read it aloud). Some have said that alliterative, repetitive prayers like this were used by those who attempted to enter a trance-like or meditative state in prayer. The words themselves were not as important as the rhythm. *Kaddish* is another example of the type of rhythmic repetitive prayer.

- The *tzitzit* are released and kissed after "*la-ad kay-ya-met*" (release them after the word "*kay-ya-met*" in that sentence.)
- This blessing continues with several allusions as to how God has helped us, rescued us (from Egypt) and redeemed us.
- The word "*emet*" is repeated several times here highlighting, almost as a staccato the "truth" of these paragraphs.

The section continues with *mi-khamokha* (who is like you *Adonai?*). The fact that the exodus from Egypt is such an important part of the daily Jewish conscience is reflected by the recitation of the most well-known part of the *shirat ha-yam* (the song of the sea), the *mi-khamokha* phrase – twice per day, every day. Many scholars have referred to the exodus as a sort of Israelite Independence Day. The beginning of our peoplehood is truly the exodus from Egypt. People who have had personal exoduses in life, whether it might be moving to start a new job, getting out of a dangerous situation, or even something as simple as leaving the confines of a sports stadium, know the feeling of comfort that an exodus has created. How much more so when the Israelites are freed from slavery?

Practice a melody

This section surrounding the *Sh'ma* concludes with *tzur yisrael* (can practice a melody here as well) and the final *brakha* of *ga'al yisrael*, we praise God for redeeming Israel.

~~

Explain the Nature of a Learner's Service and Our Method at each session:

- We will explore and discuss various prayers and service elements
- We'll take an in-depth look at one part of the service each session but experience a "complete" service each time.

**SESSION #3:
THE TORAH SERVICE**

THIS SESSION: THE TORAH SERVICE

A general comment to participants before beginning – reinforce at each session.

Page announcements let you know where the prayer leader is reading. **You do not need to be on the same page or even within the same prayer. Take your time, focus on a word, a phrase, a thought. You do not need to read or say every word of the service.** The *siddur* is like a great museum. There are numerous masterpieces within but you never expect to see them all in one visit.

Preparation:

For many of us, our main experience with *Shabbat* morning services is the Torah service.

We often arrive during this portion of the service to hear the Bar or Bat Mitzvah chant, or to listen to the Rabbi's sermon.

Actually there is little active participation by the congregation for this often-large block of time.

How many of you have felt disconnected, bored or distracted?

Rabbi Louis Finkelstein once said "When I pray, I speak to God, when I study Torah, God speaks to me". Have YOU heard God's voice during these times?

If not, how can this change?

How many have been offered an *aliyah* and turned it down feeling uncertain about your abilities?

Part 1: Introductory Prayers and Removing the Torah from the Ark

Structure of the Torah Service:

Part 1: Introductory Prayers and Removing the Torah from the Ark

Part 2: Torah Reading

Part 3: *Haftarah* Reading

Part 4: Various Prayers (community, country, etc.)

Part 5: Concluding Prayers and returning the Torah to the Ark

Ein kamokha, av ha-rahamim. Praise for God and prayer for a rebuilt Jerusalem

Va-ye'hi binsoah ha'aron – The congregation rises as the Ark is opened. "With the moving of the Ark, Moses would say, 'Arise, Adonai so that your enemies be scattered…Blessed in the One who gave Torah.'"

The rabbis of old were uncomfortable with references to war and fighting (cf. the real story of *Hanukah*). Yet despite this, the authors of the early *siddur* incorporated a war text into the Torah service. When the Israelites would march into war, the Levites would hoist up the *mishkan* (portable sanctuary) and carry it into battle. Just imagine the sight of this as you are one of the nations that God commanded that the Israelites battle? It might promote fear in the enemy yet at the same time confidence for the Israelites. "*Adonai!* Scatter your foes, so that Your enemies flee Your Presence."

B'rikh shemeh. Another statement of God's glory and mercy, this time in Aramaic. Many congregations chant the last two phrases together "*beh ana ra-khetz.*" Practice a tune for this with the group.

After the Torah is removed, the Ark is closed.

Reader continues with *Sh'ma Yisrael* and *ehad eloheinu* each of which are repeated by the congregation. Reader concludes with *gadlu* while facing the Ark and bowing. The congregation bows as well. Again all three are variations on praise and acknowledgement of God.

In most communities, there is a procession with the Torah through the congregation, moving clockwise.

As the Torah is carried in procession we chant phrases from the book of Chronicles and Psalms. Congregants often touch the Torah with the fringes on their tallit or with their siddur and then kiss the fringe or the siddur. This enables each person to make a ***personal connection with the Torah.***

The Torah is placed on the reading table and the congregation is seated.

The weekly reading is broken down into seven sections. Some congregations read the entire *parsha* (reading for that week) each week, others read one-third each week progressing on a three-year cycle, known as the triennial cycle.

The reading of each section is introduced by a blessing read by the person honored to have an "*aliyah*".

Review the blessings. Note in particular the tenses in the two verbs in these blessings. At first God is described as having given us the Torah (i.e. *natan lanu,* in the past), but in the final line of the blessing God is described as "*notein ha-Torah*", Giver of the Torah, i.e. ***in the present tense.*** The message is that not only has God given us the Torah in the past; God gives it to us as new every time that we read it. ***God's "revelation" was not a static event at Mount Sinai but a continuous process.***

Part 2: Torah Reading

Practical Tips for Having an *Aliyah* (refer to the FJMC video)

Consider a "group *aliyah*" for this session. Teach the skills

> Be prepared to come to the *bima* – move up to the front row beforehand
>
> The Torah reader will show you where the reading begins. Touch that place with your *tallit* or with your *siddur* and then kiss the *tallit* or *siddur*.
>
> It is customary to hold onto the wooden handles of the Torah during the *aliyah* blessing ("it is a tree of life for those who grasp it…") and to continue to hold the right handle for the duration of the *aliyah*.
>
> The reader will show you where the reading has ended. Again, touch that spot with *tallit* or *siddur,* which you then kiss.
>
> After the final blessing, move to stand next to the *Gabbai* on the left, who will show you exactly where to stand, and remain there for the next reading. This gives honor to the Torah by your not rushing off.
>
> It is customary for congregants to offer you congratulations. Many will say "*yishar koach*" or "*yasher koach*" (i.e. more power to you). The traditional reply is *Barukh ti-hi-yeh* (may you be blessed).

Prayer for Healing

Many congregations will pause and invite congregants to offer names as a prayer for healing is read. This usually takes place between two of the *aliyot*. It is traditional, although not required, to use the person's Hebrew name with the mother's name instead of the traditional use of the father's Hebrew name. In some communities, both parents names are used. It is also fine to use the person's English name. Be sure that the person or their family knows that they have been remembered in your prayers. It is SO important to acknowledge them.

Hagbah/Gelilah

After the final *aliyah*, the Torah is raised by the person honored to be "*hagbah*" and wrapped by the "*gelilah*".

Consider offering a session on these skills at another time.

Part 3: *Haftarah* Reading

Reading of the *Haftarah* is an honor often given to a *Bar Mitzvah* or to mark other special occasions. These selections come from the books of the prophets.

The reading is preceded and followed by blessings.

Note how the melody (*trop*) for these readings differs from that for reading the Torah.

Part 4: Various Prayers

The *siddur* includes a variety of prayers that may be read here. These include:

- Prayers to honor those who have had aliyot, for the bar mitzvah
- Prayers for the community
- Prayers for the government of the country
- Prayers for the State of Israel
- Prayers for Safety of Armed Forces
- Prayers for Peace

Concluding Prayers of this section

Before the Torah is returned to the Ark, *Ashrei* is said. Remind participants about the tradition of saying *Ashrei* three times a day ensuring a place in the World to Come. This is the second time (the first is in *shacharit*, the third is in *Minhah*)

Part 5: Returning the Torah to the Ark:

There is a remarkable symmetry between the process for taking the Torah from the Ark and replacing it.

The prayer leader holds the Torah, and chants words of praise and the congregation responds.

The Torah is then carried through the congregation (starting to the left this time).

The congregation again chants excerpts from psalms.

The Torah is placed in the Ark while we chant "*U'v'nucho yo-mar*" "When the Ark was set down, Moses would say, Return *Adonai*, you and your glorious Ark, return to dwell among the multitudes of Israel."

We conclude the Torah service with "*Etz chayim*"; It is a tree of life for those who hold on to it.

Practice a melody.

~~

Explain the Nature of a Learner's Service and Our Method at each session:
- We will explore and discuss various prayers and service elements
- We'll take an in-depth look at one part of the service each session but experience a "complete" service each time.

A general comment to participants before beginning – reinforce at each session.

Page announcements let you know where the prayer leader is reading. **You do not need to be on the same page or even within the same prayer. Take your time, focus on a word, a phrase, a thought. You do not need to read or say every word of the service.** The siddur is like a great museum. There are numerous masterpieces within but you never expect to see them all in one visit.

SESSION #4: P'SUKAI D'ZIMRA

This Session: *P'sukei D'Zimra* - **A Warm-up of Psalms and Songs**

Preparation:

Today we are talking about the warm-up. Take a moment to pause and think about how you prepare to engage in a task. Ask for some examples of warm-ups. Some could include:

> The athlete who stretches before taking the field.
>
> Other athletes who listen to a piece of music before leaving the locker room.
>
> The musician who plays scales (or the singer who sings them).
>
> Others.

A Few Comments:

You don't need to recite everything. It is likely that this section was originally composed of only the beginning and concluding blessing, and perhaps *Ashrei*, and has since expanded to current levels.

Some find that humming or doing a little *niggun* during this section is meaningful or gets them into the right mood for prayer.

The *hallel*. You have all heard of "the *hallel*" a unit of psalms that are said on holidays and at the Passover *Seder*. But originally this term, hallel meant any set of psalms of praise. The core of the *p'sukei d'zimra* is another *hallel* - the "daily *hallel*".

The five psalms that conclude this section are the final five in the book of Psalms. Reading them in this manner is like reading the entire book of psalms every day. The psalms are considered to be the apex of divinely-inspired writing. Within 150 texts we find a vast range of emotions: love; hate; fear; submission to God; asking the unanswerable questions; bravado. They truly reflect the human experience. When the early *siddur* was being created, perhaps the authors recognized that not only was it unnecessary to create entirely new texts, but that they could not do better than the psalms. They carefully chose ones that helped create the mood that they were looking for, and were specific about the order. As one progresses through the psalms in *p'sukei d'zimra* and *shacharit*, they move us closer and closer to the mental state that was the goal to be able to approach God in prayer.

Focus on *Barukh She-amar*.

- Congregation rises through the first paragraph.

- Read the English.

- Note *barukh she-amar* - Blessed is the One who spoke (past tense).

- The remainder of the prayer is in the present tense. Look around you. The world is being re-created every day. One of the reasons that it is customary to pray in a space with windows is so that we can appreciate the wonders of the creation that we are acknowledging here.

- "Blessed is the one who spoke; a reference to creation BUT

- *Our* speech creates as well. It can create-friendships and relationships, and we can also destroy through evil speech.

- The second line and last lines form "*barukh hu..u'baruch shemo*" ("Blessed is God and blessed is God's name").

Spend time on *Ashrei*.

- The beginning is actually psalm 84, the final verse of psalm 144, and then all of psalm 145.

- The sages say that anyone who recites this psalm three times a day is assured of a place in the world to come.

- A key phrase of this psalm is "*po-teyach et ya-dekha, u-masbee-a l'khol chai rahtzon*", "You open your hand and satisfy every living being with favor". Some mirror this phrase by extending and opening their own hand.

- Some add their own *kavanah* or personal intention of imitating God's ways by quoting the Talmud: "As God clothes the naked, so must you clothe the naked. As God visited the sick, so must you visit the sick" and therefore as God sustains those who are hungry, so must we. Look at the English. (Talmud - *Sotah* 14a)

- Point out the parallel with the first line and *ma-tovu: Ma-tovu ohalekha* (how goodly are your tents) and *Ashrei yoshvei vetechka* (happy are they who dwell in your house). You might think of *ma tovu* as said when you walk into *shul, ashrei* when you sit down.

The *p'seukei d'zimra* ends, as it begins with a blessing- "*yish-tabah*".

We rise here as we did at the beginning of the section for the concluding *brakha* of the section.
Some call this the "blessing of song" – "*birkat hashir*" since it concludes "Blessed are you, God….Lord of wonders who chooses melodious songs…"

~~

SESSION #5: BIRKHOT HA-SHACHAR

Explain the Nature of a Learner's Service and Our Method at each session:

- We will explore and discuss various prayers and service elements
- We'll take an in-depth look at one part of the service each session but experience a "complete" service each time.

A general comment to participants before beginning – reinforce at each session.
Page announcements let you know where the prayer leader is reading. **You do not need to be on the same page or even within the same prayer. Take your time, focus on a word, a phrase, a thought. You do not need to read or say every word of the service.** The siddur is like a great museum. There are numerous masterpieces within but you never expect to see them all in one visit.

This Session: Warm-up to Tefilah - Birkhot Ha-Shachar – the Morning Blessings

Preparation:

Think about waking up in the morning.

- Do you have a pattern?
- Do you jump right out of bed?
- Lie there for a while thinking about the day?
- Spend time with your spouse?

Contemplate about the added meaning that can enrich your day if you also start it with acknowledging God's blessings for us.

Background:

It is hard to make the transition from the distractions of the usual morning routine to giving yourself over to prayer. Two "warm-up sections" were added to the core service to ease this transition.

Mention early part of *siddur*. This is "waking up".

Walk through the words of *modeh ani*.

Tallit. – Mention how some wrap themselves totally inside their *tallit* before reciting the appropriate *brakha*. Consider reading A *Tallit* Poem, by Yehuda Amichai *z'l*,

> Whoever put on a tallit when he was young will never forget;
> Taking it out of the soft velvet bag, opening the folded shawl
> Spreading it out, kissing the length of the neckband (embroidered
> or trimmed in gold). Then swinging it in a great swoop overhead
> like a sky, a wedding canopy, a parachute. And then winding it
> around his head as in hide-and-seek, wrapping
> his whole body in it, close and slow, snuggling into it like the cocoon
> of a butterfly, then opening would-be wings to fly.

Mention the "bathroom prayer" – *asher yatsar…b'khokhmah*. We view this routine act as so natural that we take it for granted. That is exactly why the *siddur* includes this blessing - to be mindful of life's gifts and not take even the most commonplace for granted.

The *birkhot ha-shachar* (morning blessings) is the perfect place to stop and look around. We start each day with a fresh slate; a new appreciation for the things that we might take for granted.

It is traditional to rise when the *shaliah tzibur* (prayer leader) reads these *brakhot* in the synagogue and to reply "*amen*" after each one.

Review the individual blessings and how they mirror the process of getting up, putting on clothes, etc.

Heschel coined the phrase "radical amazement". How is it possible to see what we see, experience what we experience, to live; and not be amazed?

Peter Davidson, a modern poet, gives us this sense in different words:
> There's only one surprise
> To be alive---and that
> May be forgotten daily
> If daily not remembered.

Ribon kol ha-olamim - Master of All Worlds, is a two-part prayer. The first section reminds us that we are creatures with weaknesses and faults. The second section which starts with a dramatic "*Aval*" (But; Yet) reminds us that we are chosen by God for greatness as were our ancestors. The prayer ends with a recitation of the *Sh'ma* (placed here some say to thwart the authorities in Babylonia where recitation of the *Sh'ma* was prohibited at one time.)

~~

SESSION #6: PUTTING IT ALL TOGETHER

Explain the Nature of a Learner's Service and Our Method at each session:

- We will explore and discuss various prayers and service elements

- We'll take an in-depth look at one part of the service each session but experience a "complete" service each time.

A general comment to participants before beginning – reinforce at each session.

Page announcements let you know where the prayer leader is reading. **You do not need to be on the same page or even within the same prayer. Take your time, focus on a word, a phrase, a thought.** You do not need to read or say every word of the service. The siddur is like a great museum. There are numerous masterpieces within but you never expect to see them all in one visit.

Putting it all together for one complete service:
This session should be a joyous celebration of all that has been accomplished during this series.

Conduct the service, from start to finish, including plenty of *ruach*!

Attendees should be invited as special guests to attend the congregational *kiddush* as tribute to their accomplishments.

Encourage them to continue to attend on *Shabbat* morning on some regular basis.

Also encourage formation of a "buddy system" so that no one feels alone when they enter the main sanctuary or join another service in the community.

WHY AN ALTERNATIVE SERVICE?

THE FACTS

The vast majority of North American Conservative/Masorti synagogues fail to attract a significant percentage of their congregation to Shabbat morning services. According to recent data, fewer than five percent of affiliated Conservative synagogue members attend *Shabbat* morning services regularly (at least once a month). If an individual doesn't attend services the likelihood that they will have a *Shabbat* experience will be less. In order to encourage our members to have a more meaningful *Shabbat* experience, a vibrant engaging alternative service might attract them.

THE CHALLENGES

Shabbat morning services last from two and a half to three hours and are primarily conducted in Hebrew. Obviously they appeal most to those who are familiar with the service. However, a Hebrew service is a challenge to those who are not familiar with the meaning, cadence and structure of the service. Given this reality, they find it difficult to pray. In addition the Torah and *Haftarah* segments, which add at least forty-five minutes to an hour to the service, are often misunderstood or a distraction. These factors are just some of the reasons why attendance is diminishing, and engagement and meaning are wanting.

The traditional service at best provides a minimal opportunity to learn prayer skills or to achieve a better understanding of the structure and beauty of the prayer service. There is an untapped and unsatisfied yearning in the hearts of many of our congregants to have a *Shabbat* morning experience but this desire is hindered by what our congregations are providing.

I have created an Interpretive/Experiential *Shabbat* service to address these concerns. It is not a learners' service. It is designed for adults, regardless of whether they are literate in Hebrew, who wish to create and share a community *Shabbat* morning prayer experience, and who wish to improve their understanding of *Shabbat,* prayer and Torah.

This service has been meeting at Congregation Beth Judea in Long Grove, Illinois for the past three years. The leadership of my synagogue, clergy and lay, were initially concerned that a small group of congregants who regularly attended the primary service might be drawn away. It took more than two years, and a clear demonstration that the individuals promoting the alternative service were not already regular attendees, for synagogue leadership to agree to the creation of an alternative service. The new prayer community began with four individuals and has grown to more than thirty. They meet on the first and third *Shabbatot* of each month. Very few regular attendees of

THE INTERPRETIVE/ EXPERIENTIAL SHABBAT MORNING PRAYER SERVICE
BY NORM KURTZ

the main service attend. Congregation leadership recognizes that the *minyan* attracts and provides a different group of men and women a meaningful Shabbat morning prayer experience.

It is assumed that people using this module will adapt its content and customize its format to their own communities.

OBJECTIVES:

- To create a warm and welcoming prayer community.

    Before the service begins we welcome new members, go around the room and introduce ourselves. Each person updates the group about our family or something else of newsworthiness. We schmooze for about five to ten minutes.

- To develop a service which conforms to the rituals and traditions of Conservative Judaism.

    The service is abbreviated, but includes the salient and required portions of every Shabbat morning service.

- To present a service which is accessible and non-threatening regardless of the level of Hebrew language fluency or of prayer familiarity.

    Most of the prayers are recited in Hebrew and in English.

- To assure that the opportunity to learn and to develop prayer skills and Torah knowledge occurs each Shabbat morning.

    We encourage questions and discussion throughout the service. The last half hour or so is devoted to an open discussion about the Torah portion of the week.

- To provide the opportunity to integrate into the established minyan for the conclusion of the service and for the community kiddush.

    This enables the members of the alternative minyan to participate in musaf, hear the Rabbi's weekly comments, to sing the concluding prayers and to recite mourner's kaddish (if necessary) with the entire congregation. Most importantly, it emphasizes that this service is not separate from the congregation, but is an alternative Shabbat morning experience offered by the congregation.

SERVICE OVERVIEW

The service provides a comfortable environment to explore and participate in prayer, learn Torah and experience community. There is no dress code, newcomers are welcomed and questions and discussion are encouraged during the course of the service (just like during a Passover *Seder*). The emphasis is on creating a shared experience meaningful to each individual. It is of secondary importance that we "finish" every word of the service.

The service leader introduces him/herself and encourages each in attendance to introduce themselves and to spend a moment or two sharing whatever is on their mind from the prior or coming week. The purpose of this "sharing" is to create a community with personal bonds. We sit in a circle. This makes the experience less formal and supports the desired atmosphere.

When a *minyan* is present, the occasion is marked by a recitation of the *she'hecheyanu* blessing (commemorating joy of the occasion) in order to strengthen the sense of community. Sometimes we sanctify the presence of a quorum of ten individuals with joy and celebration, with a *brakha* and a cup of wine.

The service leader explains that, although this is not a learners' *minyan*, questions or comments are always invited and appropriate. If the service is not completed as outlined, we all agree that it is more important to share than to stick to the script. Our mantra is that we treat the service as a Passover *Seder* – questions are invited, conversation is encouraged, and some levity is always welcome. Everyone has a chance to lead, whether in English or in Hebrew. Our rule (not hard and fast) is whatever is recited in Hebrew is also recited in English. Individuals are encouraged to extend their comfort zone and learn new parts of the service to lead. We use familiar melodies to encourage participation.

The service lasts for one hour and fifteen minutes. It begins at 10:30 and concludes by 11:45. The first thirty to forty minutes is devoted to prayer. The remaining time focuses on a discussion of the Torah portion.

THE RIGHT LEADER

It is critical that the service leader understands this is not just about leading a service – this is about creating a supportive and welcoming minyan affording those who, for whatever reason, are uncomfortable with the traditional service, the opportunity to worship in a non-threatening, sharing, caring, learning and supportive environment. The personality of the leader, the leader's prayer skills, and the leader's level of knowledge are equally important to the *minyan's* success.

SERVICE OUTLINE

The prayer portion of the service is a "bullet point" service, meaning that it covers the bare essentials of the introductory and *shacharit* services without compromising the integrity or the traditions of those services. Each selection was chosen, not randomly, but with a specific purpose. The outline that follows is what usually occurs in the *minyan*.

INTRODUCTORY SECTION

Ma tovu. This prayer connotes community. We recite only the first sentence of this prayer, which is from the Numbers, Chapter 22, and is the story of the diviner Balaam. When the King, Balak, asks Balaam to curse the People of Israel, Balaam refuses. Rather, he is awestruck by the perceived cohesiveness and harmony of the encampment he sees and blesses the People of Israel. When we join in a *minyan* for prayer we are reminded of the importance and supportive value of participating in a prayer community.

BIRKHOT HA-SHACHAR
The Morning Blessings

Birkhot ha-shachar. The list of the morning blessings. We read each line in Hebrew and then in English. These morning blessings begin to shape the reflective focus we are to achieve with each day's morning prayers. The word, "to pray", in the Hebrew, is a reflective verb, and thus, it is meant to cause us to self-judge as we recite the prayers. The Torah teaches that we are created in the image of God ("*b'tzelim elohim*"). By praising God in prayer we gain a better understanding of what we are instructed to do through the *mitzvot* by reflecting not only on those things done by God for which we are grateful, but on those actions which we might do to come closer to the type of human being God envisioned by creating us in God's image.

Psalm for *Shabbat* (Psalm 92) – We recite in English responsively and then sing or recite the last few lines in Hebrew beginning with the words "*tzadeek ka-tamar*". During this portion of the *birkhot ha-shachar* a specified psalm is selected for each day of the week or for each special occasion. Psalm 92 is rich with beautiful metaphors and is the psalm selected for the *Shabbat*.

P'SUKEI D'ZIMRA –
Selections of Songs

Barukh she-amar. The prayer at the beginning of the *p'sukei d'zimra* section (songs and selections) begins the warm-up portion of the service, and was inserted to help us to prepare spiritually, emotionally and mentally for the *shacharit* service. This prayer we recite in full in Hebrew and in English (both can be said responsively). The reader is drawn by the language of praising God in song and in psalm. The word "*barukh*" is repeated thirteen times recalling the thirteen attributes of God. Tying into the theme created by the *birkhot ha-shachar*, as we reflect on those things we might do to come closer to the type of human being God envisioned by creating us in God's image, we remember the thirteen attributes of God set forth in the book of Exodus. We cite the virtuous qualities of compassion, mercy, justice, and slowness to anger and reflect on our own lives and judge ourselves accordingly.

Ashrei. We first recite the first two lines in Hebrew then the entire selection responsively in the English, and we conclude with the final two lines in Hebrew. (Sometimes we'll recite the entire psalm in Hebrew responsively, depending upon if one of the congregants volunteers to lead). Since the *p'sukei d'zimra* is to be comprised of songs and psalms, this is the psalm we have chosen. In our tradition the *Ashrei* psalm has been elevated above the others and we are instructed to recite it three times a day. There are many explanations as to why this is so. One that ties into the theme already mentioned is that the psalm included language praising God's virtuous attributes, similar to the *birkhot ha-shahar*.

Others songs and psalms can be added at this point. *Shirat ha-yam*, the song of crossing the sea, is often sung at this time.

Yish-tabah – This is the final selection of the *p'sukei d'zimra* section, which we recite in full in Hebrew and in English. This poetic selection again emphasizes that we praise God with song and psalm.

Hatzi kaddish.

If there is a minyan, we recite the *barkhu.*

K'riyat Sh'ma. The *K'riyat Sh'ma* consists of three blessings that envelop the *Sh'ma* and its accompanying three passages from Torah. The themes of the blessing progress from Creation to Revelation to Redemption.

> The first blessing before the *Sh'ma* – Praising God as our Creator.
>
> *Eil adon* – We sing the *eil adon* poem, in Hebrew and in English, which helps us rediscover the wonderment of creation.
>
> Conclusion of first blessing before the *Sh'ma* – Also praising God as our Creator.
>
> The second blessing before the *Sh'ma* – We recite the entire selection in English and the last few lines in Hebrew. This is a prayer about God's love for us through Torah and our demonstration of love for God through the study of *mitzvot* and the doing of God's commandments (*mitzvot*). It sets the stage for the recital of the *Sh'ma* which is the ultimate affirmation of our acknowledgement and love of our one God and of our firm commitment to observe the *mitzvot*.
>
> *Sh'ma and v'ahavta* – We recite in Hebrew and in English
>
> *Sh'ma* – Second paragraph – We read silently.

SHACHARIT

K'RIYAT SH'MA

HA-TEFILAH - The Prayer (AMIDAH)

Sh'ma – We recite the third paragraph In English and Hebrew, kissing the *tzitzit* (fringes on the *tallit* – prayer shawl) when the word "*tzitzit*" is said.

Mi-khamokha and tzur yisrael – We recite these prayers in Hebrew and in English in preparation for the *Amidah*. By reciting the third blessing of the *K'riyat Sh'ma* we recall the exodus from Israel, we yearn for eventual redemption, and we acclaim God as the redeemer.

Amidah – This is the time for each congregant's individual conversation with God. Dependent on whether there is a *minyan*, we either recite completely to ourselves or we sing the first two pages through the *kedushah* aloud and the balance to ourselves. This we do only in Hebrew, since the individual reading can be done in Hebrew or in English.

TORAH SERVICE

TORAH READING

Because it is a *mitzvah* to hear the Torah read communally on Shabbat morning, we have a skilled Torah reader chant a few lines of the Torah portion. Usually we choose the lines that will be the focus of our discussion.

THE TORAH DISCUSSION

This part of our service normally takes between 30 and 40 minutes. After the prayer portion of the service, and after a few lines of Torah are chanted, we discuss the Torah portion of the week. Because we have found that many of those choosing to attend this *minyan* are experiencing reading Torah as an adult for the first time, the discussion is on whatever level the group finds comfortable. The "regulars" to the Interpretive/Experiential *minyan* become motivated to read the Torah portion ahead of time and prepare some talking points for the discussion.

Some suggestions:

Encourage attendees to read the entire Torah portion before coming to the service.

Recite the mitzvah blessing "*la'asok b'divrei* Torah" (to delve into the Torah) before the discussion and recite the *kaddish d'rabbanan* at the conclusion.

Do not make this a lecture – encourage participation from as many individuals as possible. Remember, the discussion is on whatever level the group finds comfortable.

Feel free to include (or substitute) a discussion of the *haftarah* reading for that week as well. Keeping in mind that one of the objectives here is to keep the length of the service to less than an hour and a half, the *haftarah* is not chanted. See the Appendix for resources for these conversations.

If the Interpretive/Experiential minyan attracts ten or more people on occasion we might forego joining the main service and conclude on our own depending upon the following:

- Whether the rabbi will be giving a drash or sermon at 11:45;
- Whether the *minyan* leader sees that the Torah discussion will lend itself to a longer conversation;
- The preference of the group whether or not to join the customary *minyan* for musaf and the concluding prayers (*ein k'eloheinu, aleinu* and *adon olam*).

Flexibility is the key in order to satisfy as many of the objectives of the *minyan* as possible.

MUSAF AND CONCLUDING PRAYERS

~~

The Interpretive/Experiential *minyan* attracts those seeking a *Shabbat* morning prayer experience and who are uncomfortable attending the traditional service. It is an appealing comfortable alternative, a welcoming portal into *Shabbat* morning prayer and weekly Torah study. This option welcomes the seeker to the benefit of the individual and the community.

Without alternatives to the traditional service, many of our members lose the opportunity to have a meaningful *Shabbat* morning prayer experience. People are less and less willing to devote two or three hours for something that does not resonate as meaningful or spiritual. The *Shabbat* morning prayer service, no matter the format, is a wonderful opportunity to build a faith community.

CONCLUSION

~~

APPENDIX

❖ References for further reading to enhance and personalize the programming at your synagogue

❖ Listing of the order of the prayers of the Shabbat service

FOR FURTHER READING

These are some of the materials that were used to prepare this manual. There are many other resources as well. Feel free to supplement this list.

Texts, Guides and Commentaries:

My People's Prayer Book. Series edited by Lawrence Hoffman, published by Jewish Lights Publishing. Each volume focuses on a specific portion of the liturgy.

Higher and Higher-Making Jewish Prayer Part of Us. Steven M. Brown, published by United Synagogue.

Entering Jewish Prayer: A Guide to Personal Devotion and the Worship Service. Rabbi Reuven Hammer. Schocken. 1995.

To Pray As A Jew: A Guide To The Prayer Book And The Synagogue Service. Hayim H. Donin. Basic Books. 1991.

Siddurim with Commentaries:

Or Hadash: A Commentary on Siddur Sim Shalom for Shabbat and Festivals. Rabbi Reuven Hammer, editor. The Rabbinical Assembly and United Synagogue. 2003.

The Koren Sacks Siddur. Rabbi Jonathan Sacks, Koren Publishing Co. Prayer-by-prayer commentary. 2009.

Siddur Lev Shalem. Rabbi Edward Feld, editor. To be published by The Rabbinical Assembly in 2015, with many excellent commentaries as well as numerous supplemental readings.

Ani Tefilla Shabbat Siddur: The Lobel Edition. A Shabbat Siddur for Reflection, Connection and Learning. Koren Publishing Co.

Siddur Eit Ratzon. Joseph Rosenstein, Shiviti Publications. 2008.

Some congregations make an enlarged copy of the list on the next page and tape it to the wall so participants can follow along, including the page numbers particular to the siddur being used by everyone.

SHABBAT SERVICE: ORDER OF PRAYERS

PRELIMINARY SERVICE: The warm-up

Birchot ha-shachar: Morning blessings
Restoration of the soul: *modeh ani; elohai neshama*
Daily blessings (standing)
Torah study
Kaddish d'rabbanan
Mizmor shir (Psalm 30)
Mourner's kaddish

P'SUKEI D'ZIMRA: The warm-up continues with verses of song

Barukh she-amar (standing)
Excerpts from Chronicles and Psalms
Excerpts from Psalms (standing for Psalm 136)
Ashrei
Psalms 146-150
Other biblical excerpts (standing)
Az ya-shir: Song of the sea (standing)
Nishmat through *shokhein ad*
Yish-tabah (standing)
Hatzi kaddish

BARKHU: The call to prayer as a minyan when ten or more adults are present

Conversations about God
Barkhu (Call to Prayer-standing)

SH'MA AND ITS BLESSINGS

First blessing before: Light (includes "*eil adon*")
Second blessing before: God's love (*ahava rabba*)
Sh'ma – and its three paragraphs
First blessing after: Redemption (*ga'al yisrael*)

AMIDAH

Conversations with God
Avot: Patriarchs
G'vurot: Divine might
Kedushah: Holiness
Special Shabbat morning *brakha* paragraphs:
- *Yismach Moshe:* Moses brings the Torah
- *V'sham-ru:* Keeping the Sabbath
- *V'lo n'tato:* Sabbath uniquely given to Israel
- *R'tzei vim-nu-kha-tei-nu:* Sanctify the Sabbath

Avodah: Temple service
Modim: Thanksgiving
Sim Shalom: Peace
Closing meditation
Kaddish shalem

SHABBAT SERVICE: ORDER OF PRAYERS

TORAH READING

Opening the Ark and procession
Torah reading
Hatzi kaddish
Raising and wrapping Torah
Haftarah reading
Various prayers (congregation, country, etc.)
Ashrei
Procession and return of Torah
Hatzi kaddish

MUSAF AND CONCLUDING PRAYERS

Amidah
Kaddish shalem
Ein k'eloheinu
Aleinu
Mourner's *kaddish*
Concluding prayer (*adon olam*, etc.)

We gratefully acknowledge the contributions and insights from the following:

Hazzan Steven Dress

Hazzan Sheldon Levin

Hazzan Jeff Myers

Alex Weinberg

The FJMC mission is to involve Jewish Men in Jewish Life by building and strengthening Men's Clubs in the Conservative / Masorti Movement. We accomplish this mission by:

Leadership: mentoring leaders at the club, region and international level,

Innovation: developing programming that better connects people of all ages to the Jewish community,

Community: forming meaningful long-lasting relationships based on camaraderie, common interests and core values.

FJMC, a partnership of affiliated clubs with members across North America and around the world, brings value and adds meaning to the lives of men and their families. Through our programming and the broad dissemination of the creative programming developed by our clubs, we touch hundreds of thousands of people each year.

Website: www.fjmc.org
Facebook: FJMC_HQ
Twitter: @FJMC_HQ
LinkedIn: http://www.linkedin.com/company/fjmc
E-mail: international@fjmc.org

ISBN No. Paperback: 978-0-935665-11-6
ISBN No. E-book: 978-0-935665-12-3

© 2015

This book may not be reproduced, transmitted, or stored in whole or in part by any means, including graphic, electronic, or mechanical without the express written consent of the publisher except in the case of brief quotations embodied in critical articles and reviews.

FJMC Publications & Materials

FJMC publications are available through its website store at www.fjmc.org. Books marked with an asterisk * are available in electronic form (ex. – Kindle or Nook) through links on the FJMC site.

Biblical Leadership After Moses: Lessons to be Learned*
By Rabbi Charles Simon
"This wonderful collection of essays offers principles of effective leadership for volunteers in any organization. … these principles of leadership are clearly and persuasively detailed in a highly readable and accessible format."
Dr. Ron Wolfson, Fingerhut Professor of Education, American Jewish University
Author, Relational Judaism: Using the Power of Relationships to Transform the Jewish Community

Understanding the Haftarot: An Everyperson's Guide*
By Rabbi Charles Simon
"If the Haftarot are to reclaim their rightful place as a primary pedagogic tool for uncovering and imagining the Torah's deep truths for the modern synagogue attendee, then Rabbi Simon's exquisite, erudite and thorough introduction to the material offers an essential backdrop to each of us, clergy and layperson alike."
Aaron Alexander, Dean Ziegler School of Rabbinic Studies American Jewish University

Understanding Ma'ariv: Book & CD
Guide to leading and participating in the evening service. Includes full Hebrew text with musical notation side-by-side with English translation and transliteration.

Understanding Havdalah: Book & CD
Designed to teach anyone, even with minimal Hebraic skills, to chant Havdalah, the ceremony that separates Shabbat from the rest of the week. Includes full Hebrew text, translations and transliterations. Traditional music and the music of composer Debbie Friedman z'l.

Engaging The Non-Jewish Spouse: Strategies for Clergy and Lay Leadership
provides a step-by-step guide to inclusion taking into consideration the unique culture of each community. It suggests questions that should be discussed by a synagogue's leadership and serves as tool to further engage and guide a Board of Directors.

Intermarriage: Concepts and Strategies for Families and Synagogue Leaders*
Does Keruv have an ideology and theology? And if so what is it? This is the most current thinking about intermarriage to date, an important read for family members and community leaders who wish to effectively work with intermarrieds or potential intermarrieds.

Jewish Men at the Crossroads*
This book addresses the many issues facing modern Jewish men, intermarriage, co-parenting, sexual dysfunction, retirement, and the evolving role of men.

Hearing Men's Voices Series
A series designed to stimulate discussions and involvement in structured program activities directly related to the issues confronting Jewish men. The books are:

Work and Worth *Body and Spirit*
Our Fathers/Ourselves *Listening to God's Voice*

Tefillin
The FJMC carries affordable Kosher Tefillin for sale to encourage the performance of this Mitzvah.

www.fjmc.org

Made in the USA
Columbia, SC
26 October 2023